MY BOOK OF Stories

write your own
Myths

BRITISH LIBRARY

First published in 2016 by
The British Library
96 Euston Road
London NW1 2DB

Text copyright © Deborah Patterson 2016
Illustrations copyright © The British Library Board 2016
Additional images © Shutterstock.com

ISBN 978 0 7123 5643 5

British Library Cataloguing in Publication Data
A catalogue record for this book is available from the British Library

Designed by Perfect Bound Ltd
Picture research by Sally Nicholls

Printed in Malta by Gutenberg Press

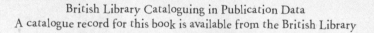

MY BOOK OF Stories

write your own Myths

BRITISH LIBRARY

Thanks to Rob and Rebecca at the
British Library for continuing to believe in
me, and the wonderful Sally for her
boundless knowledge

Contents

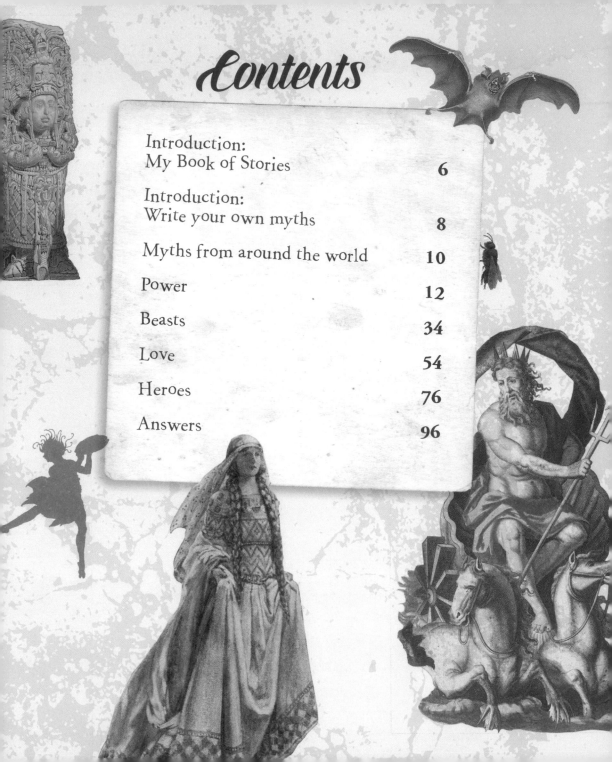

Introduction: My Book of Stories

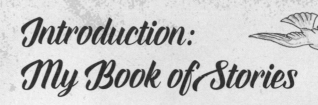

My Book of Stories is full of inspirational ways to start your own stories. Snippets of text collected from some of the best stories ever written such as *Cinderella*, *Romeo and Juliet*, and *The Wizard of Oz*, have been paired with story suggestions of how to write what happens next. Top tips on how to write a story, and lists of inspirational words used by expert authors such as Shakespeare, Lewis Carroll and J.K. Rowling will help you along your way.

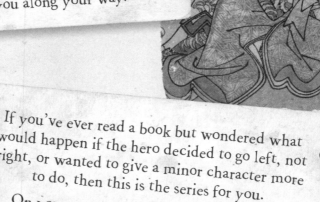

If you've ever read a book but wondered what would happen if the hero decided to go left, not right, or wanted to give a minor character more to do, then this is the series for you.

On your story writing journey you'll find fun puzzles to do, silly lists and titbits of information about authors and their books.

So you want to sit down and write some stories?

What do you need?

A pen, some paper, and then what?

You need to decide what to write about. Where do you start?

Top 5 inspirational story starters

1. Real-life stories
2. Myths and fairy tales
3. The world around you
4. A book that you've read
5. Your own interests, such as sport, music, or films

Ready to get scribbling??

Introduction:
Write your own myths

Myths are gripping stories. They contain adventure, near-death experiences and nature, in the hands of the gods, at its most raw and powerful. Heroes are made, and heroes fall. There are battles for power and there are battles in the name of love.

The stories of mythology originate in the oral tradition of storytelling, which means, at least to start with, that the stories weren't written down. Imagine telling a story round a campfire, and each time you tell it you exaggerate one exciting point and embellish another. Your friend hears your story and tells it to someone else, but adds a new character, and another friend takes the story a bit further still. There is rarely a definitive version of a myth, and that gives the storytellers lots of freedom. It also means that when you write your own myths you are becoming part of an ancient tradition of storytelling.

Within the pages of *My Book of Stories: write your own myths*, are lots of different opportunities to retell and reshape well-known myths, as well as to write new stories inspired by them. So step into the shoes of the ancients and write some gripping adventure tales.

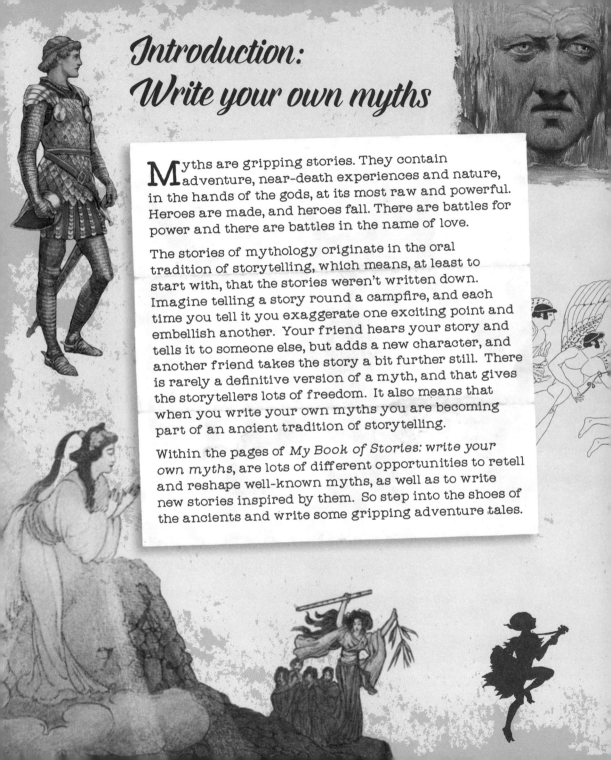

The meaning of myth

Myths are traditional stories which were told by many of the world's early cultures. The saying "That's a myth" means that something is untrue.

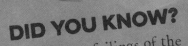

DID YOU KNOW?

The human failings of the mythological heroes of Greece and Rome inspired Rick Riordan, the author of the Percy Jackson series.

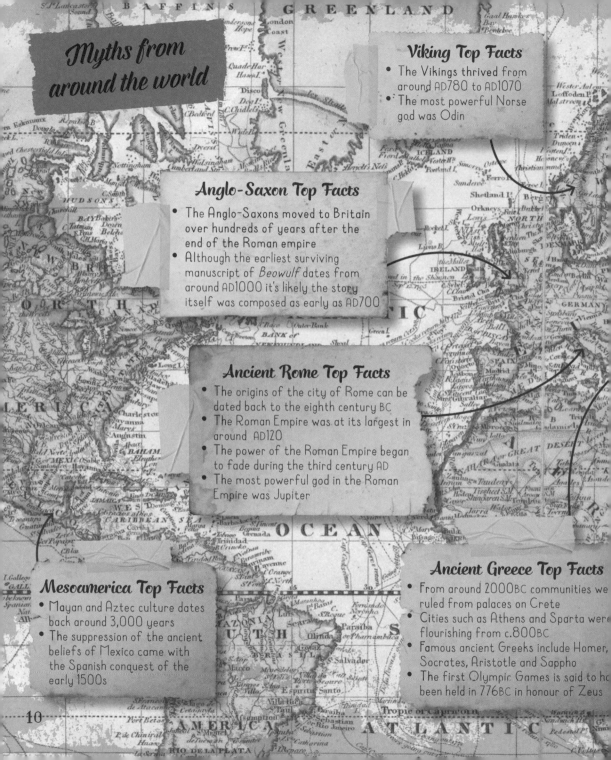

Myths from around the world

Viking Top Facts
- The Vikings thrived from around AD780 to AD1070
- The most powerful Norse god was Odin

Anglo-Saxon Top Facts
- The Anglo-Saxons moved to Britain over hundreds of years after the end of the Roman empire
- Although the earliest surviving manuscript of *Beowulf* dates from around AD1000 it's likely the story itself was composed as early as AD700

Ancient Rome Top Facts
- The origins of the city of Rome can be dated back to the eighth century BC
- The Roman Empire was at its largest in around AD120
- The power of the Roman Empire began to fade during the third century AD
- The most powerful god in the Roman Empire was Jupiter

Mesoamerica Top Facts
- Mayan and Aztec culture dates back around 3,000 years
- The suppression of the ancient beliefs of Mexico came with the Spanish conquest of the early 1500s

Ancient Greece Top Facts
- From around 2000BC communities we ruled from palaces on Crete
- Cities such as Athens and Sparta were flourishing from c.800BC
- Famous ancient Greeks include Homer, Socrates, Aristotle and Sappho
- The first Olympic Games is said to ha been held in 776BC in honour of Zeus

Ancient Mesopotamia Top Facts

- The great cities of Mesopotamia flourished from c.2334BC to c.539BC
- Most of ancient Mesopotamia can be found in modern-day Iraq
- The people of Mesopotamia included the Akkadians, the Assyrians, the Babylonians and the Sumerians
- The most powerful god in Mesopotamia was Marduk

Ancient Egypt Top Facts

- Lower Egypt and Upper Egypt were united in c.3100BC
- The ancient Egyptians revered the River Nile
- Pharaohs ruled Egypt for around 3,000 years
- Egypt became part of the Roman Empire in c.30BC

Japan Top Facts

- The mythology of Japan dates back over 2,000 years
- Shinto is the indigenous faith of Japan
- The gods of Shinto are known as kami

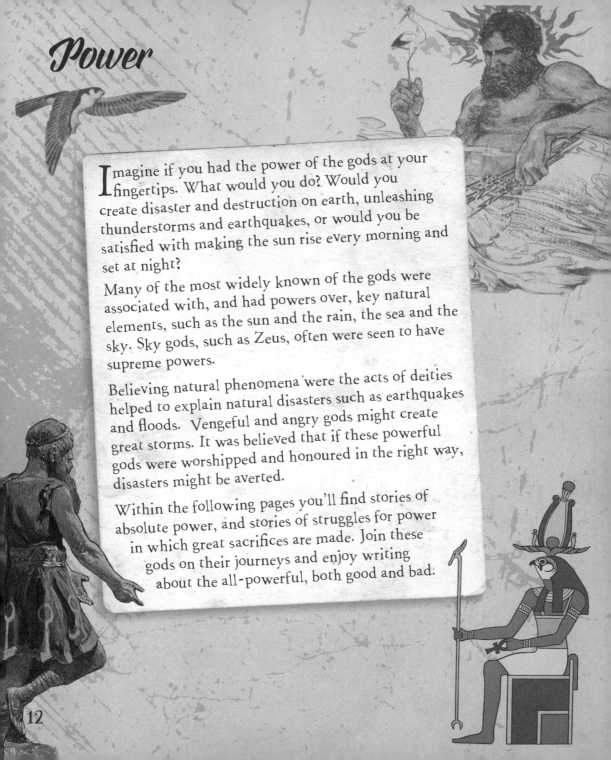

Power

Imagine if you had the power of the gods at your fingertips. What would you do? Would you create disaster and destruction on earth, unleashing thunderstorms and earthquakes, or would you be satisfied with making the sun rise every morning and set at night?

Many of the most widely known of the gods were associated with, and had powers over, key natural elements, such as the sun and the rain, the sea and the sky. Sky gods, such as Zeus, often were seen to have supreme powers.

Believing natural phenomena were the acts of deities helped to explain natural disasters such as earthquakes and floods. Vengeful and angry gods might create great storms. It was believed that if these powerful gods were worshipped and honoured in the right way, disasters might be averted.

Within the following pages you'll find stories of absolute power, and stories of struggles for power in which great sacrifices are made. Join these gods on their journeys and enjoy writing about the all-powerful, both good and bad.

Don't fight fate

Myths from different cultures often feature beings who were controllers of destiny. These gods decided at what point the life of a person started, and when, and often how that life would end. This power over life and death was usually absolute, with only the very rarest cases successful in their fight with fate.

The Twelve Olympians

The twelve most powerful deities in the Greek myths lived on Mount Olympus.

1. *Zeus, god of sky and thunder*
2. *Hera, goddess of marriage*
3. *Poseidon, god of the sea*
4. *Aphrodite, goddess of love*
5. *Athena, goddess of war and Athens*
6. *Apollo, god of healing, music and the arts*
7. *Ares, god of war*
8. *Artemis, goddess of hunting*
9. *Demeter, goddess of the Earth, grain and fertility*
10. *Hephaestus, god of fire and metalworking*
11. *Hestia, goddess of the hearth, family and domestic life*
12. *Hermes, messenger of the gods*

13

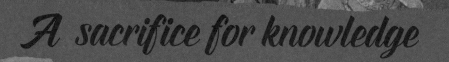

A sacrifice for knowledge

To obtain the great wisdom for which he is so famous, Odin visited Mimir's spring, "the fountain of all wit and wisdom," in whose liquid depths even the future was clearly mirrored, and asked the old man who guarded it to let him have a drink. But Mimir refused unless Odin would consent to give one of his eyes in exchange.

The god did not hesitate, so highly did he prize the liquid, but immediately plucked out one of his eyes, which Mimir kept in pledge, sinking it deep down into his fountain, where it shone with mild lustre, leaving Odin with but one eye, which is considered to be a symbol of the sun.

(*Myths of the Norsemen* by Hélène Adeline Guerber)

Rewrite this story of the Norse sky god, Odin, imagining that you have journeyed to Mimir's well on a quest for true knowledge. What does Mimir ask you to give him? Are you prepared to make the sacrifice?

Finn the Seer, a hero from the Fenian Cycle of Irish mythology, waited seven years to catch the *what* of Knowledge?

a) *Salmon*
b) *Goldfish*
c) *Whale*

15

Invent an instrument of power

The sea rose high, the thunderbolt of Zeus struck that ship, and all its company was scattered upon the waters.

(*Old Greek Folk Stories Told Anew* by Josephine Preston Peabody)

In Homer's *Iliad*, Zeus is called the "cloud-gatherer", the "lord of lightning", and "god of the storm-cloud". At the heart of his power is his weapon, a powerful thunderbolt. He can use it to kill opponents or to strike fear in those who dare anger him by making the whole sky shake. His thunderbolt was made for him by Hephaestus, god of metalworking and fire.

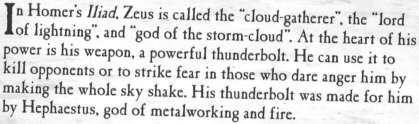

DID YOU KNOW?

Hephaestus made weapons for the gods of Mount Olympus, and for some famous mythical heroes too. Can you match the items below to their rightful owner?

Trident	Eros
Winged sandals	Athena
Arrows	Poseidon
Shield	Achilles
Armour	Hermes

Imagine that Zeus' thunderbolt is out of action. Design a new weapon for Zeus to use while his thunderbolt is fixed, and write a story in which Hephaestus gives it to Zeus, describing its powers and how to use it.

Draw a picture of the new weapon here

_____
_____
_____
_____
_____
_____
_____
_____
_____
_____
_____
_____
_____

_____
_____
_____

Wind power

Tiamat opened her mouth which was seven miles wide, and Marduk called upon the evil wind to strike her; he caused the wind to keep her mouth wide open so that she could not close it. All the tempests and the hurricanes entered in, filling her body, and her heart grew weak; she gasped, overpowered.

(*Myths of Babylonia and Assyria* by Donald Alexander Mackenzie)

When Marduk, a deity of ancient Babylon also known as Merodach, was young he was given the four winds by his grandfather as a toy to play with. His games created storms on the surface of Tiamat, the sea. Tiamat made plans to destroy the young god, but Marduk then turned the winds to his advantage and used them to destroy her.

The myths and legends of many cultures often include a god of gods, and in many cases this figure was a sky god. The Greeks had Zeus, the Romans, Jupiter. In Norse myths Odin was the leader of the three sky gods (the others were Vili and Ve). Horus was the sky god in Egyptian myths, and in Mayan culture their sky god was known simply as "Heart of the Sky". Many of these gods had enormous powers such as the ability to control thunder and lightning, the rain or the wind.

Write a story about a sky god creating a hurricane on Earth.

Try using some of these windy words in your story

hurricane
typhoon
cyclone
powerful
destruction
force
blown
angry
strong
storm
intense
eye
damage
wind
catastrophe
flooding

19

Fight for power

In gladness of heart Ra proposed a sail on the Nile, but as soon as his enemies heard that he was coming, they changed themselves into crocodiles and hippopotami, so that they might be able to wreck his boat and devour him.

As the boat of the god approached them they opened their jaws to crush it, but Horus and his followers came quickly on the scene, and defeated their plans.

(The Legends of the Gods by E.A. Wallis Budge)

The Myth of Horus and Set

Horus was the son of Osiris, King of Egypt, and Isis. Set was Osiris' brother, and a great enemy of the sun god, Ra. In the myth Set killed his brother and tried to take his place upon the throne. Horus and Set battled for eighty years. In each battle Set tried to trick Horus, but every time Horus escaped his attacks and was victorious. Eventually Ra said that Horus was the winner and named him King of Egypt.

Horus is the ancient Egyptian god of the sky and is often shown with a falcon's head. His right eye is the sun and his left eye, the moon. He is also god of war.

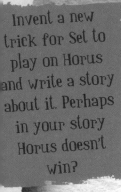

Invent a new trick for Set to play on Horus and write a story about it. Perhaps in your story Horus doesn't win?

How do we know what we know?

Myths were originally told orally, which means that they weren't written down. If this was the case, then how do we know these stories at all? With the invention of writing, people began to write down stories that they heard around them. Some stories were written as poems or plays, and others as novels or collections of short stories.

The myths of the ancient Greeks travelled with them around the Mediterranean, the Romans adapted these stories and then took them further afield. Many of the stories of the Greek gods, goddesses and heroes that we know and continue to tell today are based on the epic poems, the *Iliad* and the *Odyssey* by the poet Homer who lived around the 8th century BC.

Epic poems

- The stories of Gilgamesh, a hero of Mesopotamia, are based on an epic poem written in Akkadian around 1600 BC
- "Voluspa", "Grimnismal" and "Vafthrudnismal" are poems used by the Icelandic storyteller Snorri Sturlson in his work *The Prose Edda* from which we've learnt much about Norse myths.

We are lucky that many structures and artefacts, which are historical objects, survive from these ancient cultures which teach us a lot about how people lived in those times, and what their beliefs were. In Athens, for example, the Parthenon, which was the temple to their city's goddess, Athene, who is also known as Athena, still stands. Sculptures on the building told stories of her life and showed how she was worshipped.

Most of what we know about the myths and history of Ancient Egypt comes from the survival of sacred texts and images preserved by the desert sand. Images have been found on coffins and on the walls of tombs. It is thought that the Egyptians believed that they needed stories to aid the dead on their journey to the afterlife. A famous example of this is the *Book of the Dead*.

What is an archaeologist?

Archaeologists excavate buried remains, such as parts of buildings or artefacts, and study them to work out what they might have been. If they discover objects with marks or writing on them, they then work hard to learn what those marks mean.

Excitingly, there are parts of the ancient world which are still being uncovered. In March 2015 a group of explorers and archaeologists excavated the remains of a city in the jungle of Honduras known in legends as the 'City of the Monkey God'. They are studying sculptures found at the site to learn more about the people who lived there.

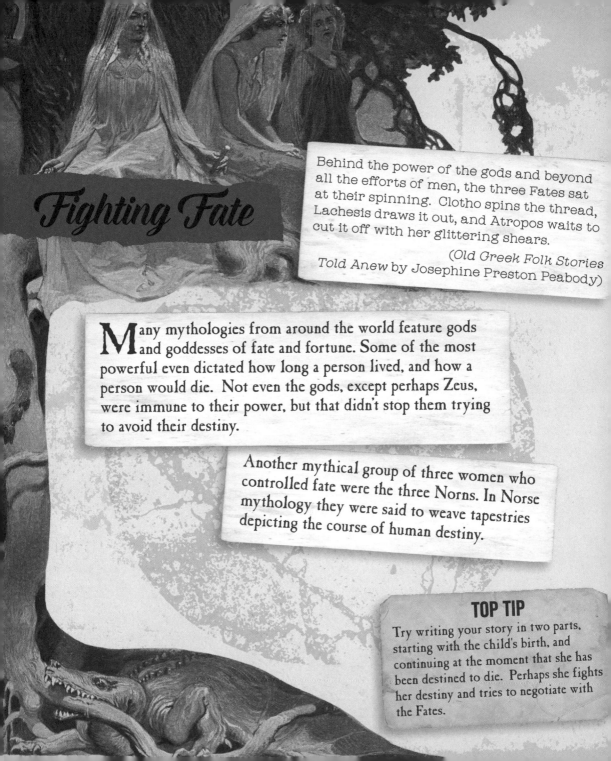

Fighting Fate

Behind the power of the gods and beyond all the efforts of men, the three Fates sat at their spinning. Clotho spins the thread, Lachesis draws it out, and Atropos waits to cut it off with her glittering shears.

(Old Greek Folk Stories Told Anew by Josephine Preston Peabody)

Many mythologies from around the world feature gods and goddesses of fate and fortune. Some of the most powerful even dictated how long a person lived, and how a person would die. Not even the gods, except perhaps Zeus, were immune to their power, but that didn't stop them trying to avoid their destiny.

Another mythical group of three women who controlled fate were the three Norns. In Norse mythology they were said to weave tapestries depicting the course of human destiny.

TOP TIP

Try writing your story in two parts, starting with the child's birth, and continuing at the moment that she has been destined to die. Perhaps she fights her destiny and tries to negotiate with the Fates.

Write a story about the three Fates arguing about the destiny of a new child.

Admetus and the Fates

The Fates, also known as the Moirai, were ready to cut the thread of life of Admetus, king of Pherae. As hope was failing, the people around him remembered the promise of the Fates to spare his life if they could find someone to die in his stead. At the last minute his queen, Alcestis, offered up her own life and prepared to die to save her husband.

25

Entice the sun goddess out of her cave

When the far-shining goddess, on account of the evil pranks of her brother, Susa no O, the Ruler of the Moon, hid herself in a cave, there was no more light, and heaven and earth were plunged into darkness.

A council of all the gods was held and the question of how to appease the anger of the goddess was discussed. A long-headed and very wise god was ordered to think out a plan to entice her forth from the cave.

(Japanese Fairy World: Stories from the Wonder-lore of Japan by William Elliot Griffis)

What happens next?

How does the council of gods decide to entice the sun goddess, also known as Amaterasu, out of her cave and bring light back to Earth?

Top 5 sun gods

1. **Apollo** was the Ancient Greek god of the sun and god of light. He was also patron of music and the arts, healing and prophecy

2. **Utu** was the Babylonian sun god. He used a saw-like knife to cut through the mountains and emerge as the dawn

3. **Ra (or Re)**, the Egyptian sun god, travelled across the sky in a solar boat

4. The Incas were known as the people of the sun and their sun god, **Inti**, was the most important of all of their deities

5. The Aztec sun god was called **Tezcatlipoca**, which means smoking mirror

> "And pray what would satisfy you?" asked the stranger.
> "It is only this," replied Midas, "I wish everything that I touch to be changed to gold!"
> (*The Golden Touch*, from *A Wonder-Book for Girls and Boys* by Nathaniel Hawthorne)

The Midas Touch

King Midas loved gold more than anything in the world, except perhaps his daughter, so when a stranger came to him and asked what would make him happiest in the world, it was natural for him to ask for the power to turn everything he touched into gold. At first he was delighted with his new power and the wealth it seemed to bring him. However, at breakfast, the cold, hard truth was made clear to him as he turned first his coffee, and then his food to gold and was unable to eat anything, and his joy evaporated completely when he accidently turned his daughter into gold when he gave her a quick kiss on the forehead. Luckily for King Midas, the stranger who had bestowed this dubious power upon him returned and gave him a way to restore everything he had touched to its original form.

The ______ Touch

Replace the word "Golden" in the title with one of the following words, then write a story that goes with it.

Woolly
Silver
Invisible
Jelly

DID YOU KNOW?

The title song of the 1964 Bond film, *Goldfinger*, includes the following lines:

"... Goldfinger
He's the man, the man with
the Midas touch ..."

Write your own story of the power of the gods

Fill these pages with your own story of gods and their extraordinary powers. Their powers can be used for both good and mischief. What will your story be about?

TOP TIP
"A fish out of water"
A good story often sees a main character in a new and unfamiliar setting, for example, the all-powerful Zeus might be living in your home town in the present day, or he could wake up one morning on Mount Olympus and find he's lost his powers. What will the "hook" be for your story?

ave a go at finding these powerful
ds and heroes in this wordsearch.

ZEUS
POSEIDON
JUPITER
SET
ODIN
ATROPOS
GILGAMESH
HORUS
MARDUK
ATHENA

A M V X K B J O Y I E O A S O
X N G I L G A M E S H T J S J
T E E I U A B M V N R W L C U
P I W H O U S S D O T T W I P
S O V A T C V V P O T D M I I
R E S V Y A M O X J B I D U T
R E T E W Z S C U M D D S T E
C Y G P I Q M G S W I D M T R
Z K G D J D C X U F B O E P N
K E M Q D A O Z R E L P A V I
P E G W T T O N O W I P V C W
K C M S O D I N H K Y L V L C
M L U Q L V M O W D A S N F U
Q E D J Y T K U D R A M G Z F
Z T F Q C W V A N C U K S Q A

Beasts

Even if you don't have your own pet at home, and even if you live in a city, it's likely that you'll see animals every day. We live with them, we work with them, and we tell stories about them. The animals in these myths are fantastical, from terrifying beasts, such as the flesh-eating swamp monster, Grendel, to half-man, half-creature hybrids, such as a centaur or a satyr.

Heroes need monsters to fight to earn their hero status. If Hercules hadn't succeeded in defeating the multi-headed Hydra, would he still be one of the most famous heroes of all time?

What would you do if you found yourself facing a goblin spider? Would you run and hide, or would you attack? When you write your own stories about these mythical beings you can be as brave as your imagination allows.

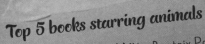
Top 5 books starring animals

1. *The Tale of Peter Rabbit* by Beatrix Potter
2. *Fantastic Mr Fox* by Roald Dahl
3. *Charlotte's Web* by E.B. White
4. *The Sheep-pig* by Dick King-Smith
5. *The Tiger Who Came to Tea* by Judith Kerr

Can you create a new hybrid creature? Draw your own head and stick it on to an animal's body. What will you call it?

Don't forget to add some of these monstrous features

claws

horns

scales

teeth

tail

fur

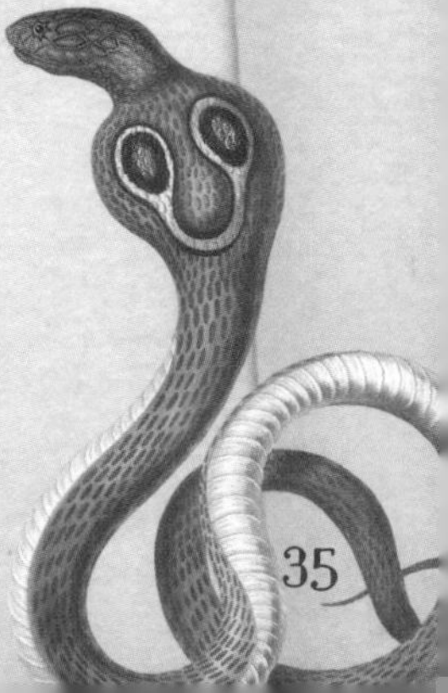

A beastly shape-changing story

From behind the rocks Aristaeus saw that Proteus slept, and on the sleep-drowsed limbs of Proteus fixed the chains that made him captive. Then, in joy and pride at having been the undoing of the shepherd of the seas, Aristaeus shouted aloud. And Proteus, awaking, swiftly turned himself into a wild boar with white tusks that he tried to thrust into the thighs of Aristaeus. But Aristaeus, unflinching, kept his firm hold of the chain.

(*The Book of Myths* by Jean Lang)

What does Proteus change into next? Is Aristaeus able to hold on to the chains?

Next Proteus changed into a

The Myth of Aristaeus and Proteus

Aristaeus, known for his bee-keeping and the honey that he collected from his hives, mistakenly angered the gods one day. They punished him by emptying his hives and killing his bees. Aristaeus sought the help of his mother, a water nymph, who told him that Proteus, a sea god known for his wisdom, was the only one who could give him the information he needed to win his bees back. The catch was that Proteus, who was able to change his shape, would only answer a question if Aristaeus was able to chain him, and hold him in those chains, no matter what beast or thing Proteus changed into.

Proteus is able to change himself into a

tiger
dragon
lion
fire
flood

What else do you think he might change into?

. . . .

. . . .

. . . .

. . . .

. . . .

. . . .

DID YOU KNOW?

The word protean, meaning versatile or able to change or adapt, comes from the name Proteus.

Man and beast

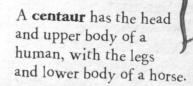

A **centaur** has the head
and upper body of a
human, with the legs
and lower body of a horse.

A **satyr** or a **faun** is half-human,
half-goat. Sometimes their human
head is depicted with goat's ears
and even horns.

A **harpy** is
half-bird and
half-woman.

A **mermaid** or **merman** has the
upper body of a human and the
lower body of a fish, and lives
beneath the waves. In Greek
mythology the god Triton
is a merman.

In many myths, where two
creatures are combined,
their attributes are
combined too. For example,
a centaur, which is half-
human and half-horse,
combines the wisdom of
the human race with the
wild nature of a horse.

Write a story inspired by the creature that you see in this picture.

_____
_____
_____
_____
_____
_____
_____
_____
_____
_____
_____
_____
_____
_____

Questions to ask yourself before you write:

■ It's half-human, but what's the other half?

■ What is it called?

■ What is its character like?

A league of demons

...as the boy was flying from the apartment he threw something at Raiko. It spread outward into a huge white sticky web, which clung so tightly to Raiko that he could hardly move. Raiko then called for assistance, and his chief servant met the miscreant and stopped his further progress with extended sword. The Goblin threw a web over him too. When he at last managed to extricate himself, he saw that Raiko had also been the victim of the Goblin Spider.

(*Myths and Legends of Japan* by F. Hadland Davis)

Create a league of demons, giving each of them a name and a special power

1. ....
2. ....
3. ....
4. ....
5. ....

The Myth of the Goblin Spider continued ...

After this attack, the Japanese hero, Raiko, was freed by his chief servant, who had escaped the web and severely wounded the Goblin Spider. The Goblin Spider was later found suffering from his wounds and was killed instantly.

A different ending

Imagine that there was a League of Demons ready to pick up where the Goblin Spider had failed. Write a comic strip about how they attempt to kill Raiko. Do they succeed or are they vanquished?

These are some animals which have scary or mysterious connotations

snake
wolf
bat
raven

What other animals can you think of?

....
....
....
....
....
....
....

TOP TIP

Usually words have to work on their own to tell a story, but in a comic strip the words and pictures can work together.

The underworld

Do you like reading scary stories? Do your favourite stories feature dragons and monsters, wizards and witches, or aliens and ghosts?

What could be more unsettling to read about than a world where demons live alongside the souls of the dead, where it's always dark, and is ruled over by a fearful god of the dead? Would you like to read a story set in that spooky place?

The Underworld, as it's often known, is that spooky place, the mythical land of the dead. Before you think you can pop down there for a look, consider these facts.

1. **It's really hard to find a way in.** The classical Underworld of the Greek myths was surrounded by the River Styx, and a ferryman, Charon, had to be paid to take souls across in his boat.

2. **You've got to get past the guards.** The entrance to this strange world was usually guarded by a demonic creature. Probably the most famous is Cerberus, the three-headed dog of Hades, but perhaps the most scary is Pazuzu, the demon of the Mesopotamian underworld who had a canine face and was covered in scales.

3. **It's full of dangers.** The Egyptians called their version of the underworld, Duat. It had familiar geographical features to the world above, but with differences too, like lakes of fire and walls of iron. There were also demons, which inhabited every corner, crevice and cavern.

4. **It's ruled over by the most feared of all the gods.** Even their names could strike fear in mere mortals. Did you know that the ruler of the Norse land of the dead was called Hel?

5. **There's no way out.** There are some stories in which extraordinary heroes such as Heracles, or the gods themselves, have been able to find a way back to the land of the living, but most mortals wouldn't stand a chance of escape.

List your top 5 scary stories

1. ....
2. ....
3. ....
4. ....
5. ....

A challenge for a modern hero

Now, in the dark fens of that land there dwelt a monster — fierce, noisome, and cruel, a thing that loved evil and hated all that was joyous and good. From its wallow in the marshes, where the deadly grey fog hung round its dwelling, the monster, known to all men as the Grendel, came forth, to kill and to devour.

(*The Book of Myths* by Jean Lang)

The story of Beowulf and Grendel is centuries old and is set in Scandinavia. Grendel attacks the grand banqueting hall of King Hrothgar after a great evening of celebration has taken place, and feasts on whomever he finds. Beowulf, the nephew of King Higelac, hears of this tragedy through a minstrel's song and comes to Hrothgar's aid, pledging to kill the monster.

Continue this story, in the present day

Choose a present-day setting from the options below to replace the king's banqueting hall and write a story of a modern hero's defeat of the terrible swamp monster, Grendel.

Football match
Television talent contest
New Year's Eve celebrations

_____
_____
_____
_____
_____
_____
_____
_____
_____

DID YOU KNOW?

Beowulf is the longest epic poem in Old English, running at over 3,000 lines long and written, it is thought, at the end of the tenth or the beginning of the eleventh century. The British Library in London houses the surviving manuscript.

Want more of a challenge? Try writing your story in poetic form, like the original.

Create a new animal god

The myths of Ancient Egypt reflected the close links between humans, domestic animals and wild animals. Their gods were given the appearance and characteristics of the animals that they encountered daily. These animal forms gave each god a clear identity.

Inspired by the animals that you encounter in your daily life, create a new animal god

Draw a picture of it here

Write its name here, including which animal it is, and what type of god it is

TOP TIP
To help you decide what your new god's character should be like, think about the animal that it is linked to. For example a fox might be wily, a dog, loyal, and an owl, wise.

Can you match the animal to the Egyptian god?

Crocodile

Cow

Falcon

Hippopotamus

Cat

Ibis

Bastet, the goddess of sexuality

Horus, the god of the sky

Taweret, the mother goddess

Thoth, the god of wisdom

Sobek, the crocodile god

Hathor, the goddess of fertility

Describe its character here:

_____

_____

_____

_____

_____

Describe how it looks here:

_____

_____

_____

_____

_____

_____

In the stars

The importance of animals to humans was reflected in stories and myths around the world. An animal of great importance to the Incas was the llama. The shape of this animal was seen in the constellation of stars known as Lyra in Europe, and was worshipped by Incan llama herders and keepers.

Write a story of discovery

Trolls, Gnomes, or Kobolds, were dark, treacherous and cunning by nature and were banished to Svart-alfa-heim, the home of the black dwarfs situated underground.

The remainder of these small creatures, including all that were fair, good, and useful, the gods called Fairies and Elves, and they sent them to dwell in the airy realm of Alf-heim, situated between heaven and earth.

(*Myths of the Norsemen* by Hélène Adeline Guerber)

The Norse trickster god, Loki, is in trouble, again. One of his tricks has gone wrong and he needs to make amends. He goes to the roots of the tree Yggdrasil, a huge ash which is the tree of the universe, in search of someone or something to help him, but he takes a wrong turn and finds himself in a new world populated by unfamiliar beings. He needs to find out if they are friend or foe, and if they are able to help him on his quest, but how will he do this?

_____
_____
_____
_____
_____
_____
_____
_____
_____
_____
_____
_____
_____
_____
_____
_____

Top 5 creatures of the Norse myths
Nidhug the dragon or serpent
The Frost Giants
Ratatosk the squirrel
The Light Elves
Trolls

Write your own beastly story

In this chapter you've met a goblin spider, a swamp-monster and monstrous creatures with human heads. Many of these are scary beasts, but imagine if they were the ones who were scared. Write a story about a demon or a beast who doesn't fit in.

Some ideas
a vegetarian vampire
a werewolf who's scared of the dark
a gentle troll

TOP TIP
Think of your story mountain. After you've introduced your characters and set the scene, present your characters with a problem. In this story your beast will need to face his fears to succeed.

3 The Problem
Your character faces his fears

2 The Build-up
Set the scene

4 Resolution
How does your character deal with the problem?

1 The Beginning
Introduce your character

5 The Ending
Did your character overcome his differences, or did his fellow beasts learn a lesson from his alternative approach?

Can you identify all of the mythical creatures, gods and monsters featured in this crossword?

Across

2. A merman who is also a sea god (6)
4. A swamp serpent with many heads, killed by Heracles (5)
7. Half-human, half-horse (7)
8. A Slavic mythical creature who drinks blood (7)
9. Egyptian crocodile god (5)

Down

1. A shape-changing sea god (7)
3. Scandinavian swamp monster (7)
5. A female monster with snakes for hair, who could turn people to stone (6)
6. A giant with one eye (7)
7. The three-headed dog who guards the Underworld (8)

Love

Love, in all of its forms, affects our lives in many ways, so it's no surprise to find gods and goddesses of love represented in mythology, and it's also no surprise that the subject of love occurs again and again in the stories. There are tales of romantic love, between gods and goddesses, and also between gods and mortals, as well as tales of parental love. There are darker tales too, with heartbreak and sad endings, such as Apollo's unrequited love for Daphne, and the forced abandonment of Romulus and Remus by their mother.

There are many goddesses of love, some who you may have heard of, and others who may be less familiar. Aphrodite, known to the Romans as Venus, is probably the most famous, alongside her son Eros, who was known to the Romans as Cupid. Cupid's arrows of desire supposedly had the power to make people fall in love.

Will these mythical tales of love and loss inspire you to create your own love stories? Will your stories have happy endings, or will they be full of woe?

Top 5 love goddesses

1. **Venus** was the Roman goddess of love and beauty
2. The Babylonian goddess of love and fertility, **Ishtar**, was known as **Inanna** in Sumerian
3. The Egyptian goddess, **Hathor**, often took the form of a cow. She was the patron of lovers, as well as the goddess of childbirth and the patron of women
4. **Freyja** was the Norse goddess associated with love. The name 'Freyja' means lady
5. **Xochiquetzal** was the Aztec goddess of love and childbirth. She was also the goddess of flowers

Hera's top 3 acts of jealousy

1. Banned the goddess Leto, who was expecting Zeus' children, from giving birth on the mainland or any island
2. Sent a fly to torment and sting Io, who had been turned into a bull
3. Tried to destroy Dionysus, son of Zeus and Semele, numerous times

Rules don't apply

The gods lived by a different set of rules to ordinary mortals, especially when it came to love and marriage. It was not just OK, but perfectly normal for a god to marry his goddess sister. It was also completely normal for both the husband and the wife to conduct affairs with other gods or mortals. That doesn't mean that everyone was happy about it. Zeus' wife, Hera, also his sister, was known for her jealousy.

DID YOU KNOW?

The second planet away from the Sun is named Venus, after the Roman goddess. It is the hottest planet in the solar system.

55

Happy families?

When Izanami had given birth to the islands, seas, rivers, herbs, and trees, she and her lord, Izanagi, consulted together, saying: "We have now produced the Great-Eight-Island country, with the mountains, rivers, herbs, and trees. Why should we not produce some one who shall be the Lord of the Universe?"

(*Myths and Legends of Japan* by F. Hadland Davis)

Izanami and Izanagi's union then produced the gods Amaterasu, the sun goddess, Tsuki yumi, the moon god, and Susa-no-o the storm god, amongst many others.

Write a story about this family of gods

_____

_____

_____

_____

_____

_____

_____

Road trip

Annual family gathering

Breakfast time

尊大戸遠尊第七 伊弉諾尊 伊弉冉尊 第六 面足尊 第五大戸道尊 第四 泥土煑尊 尊と申す 天浮橋の上に立たせて 青海原を 天瓊矛を以て 凝り固まりて ひとつの島 あぢはれり その凝り固まれるひとつの島 淡路國これなり 神 その島を大八州國と

Izanagi and Izanami are the creator gods in Japanese myths. A number of myths from around the world tell a story of Earth's creation. The stories often include descriptions of the gods who created the world, and their offspring, who are gods in their own right. Like any family, there are arguments between siblings and parents as well as love.

Agony Aunt Aphrodite

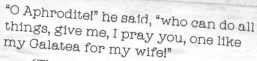

"O Aphrodite!" he said, "who can do all things, give me, I pray you, one like my Galatea for my wife!"

(*The Book of Myths* by Jean Lang)

The Myth of Pygmalion and Galatea

Pygmalion was a sculptor who once created the most beautiful sculpture of a woman. In time he came to love the woman that he had made of marble. He named her Galatea, and at the festival of Aphrodite he prayed to the goddess of love to bring his creation to life.

Aphrodite was the Greek goddess of love and was known for her beauty, and for having many lovers, both gods and mortals. She was married to Hephaestus, but had many affairs, including ones with Ares, the god of war, Hermes, the messenger to the gods, and the mortal, Adonis.

Dear Aphrodite

Write to Aphrodite with a real or imagined love problem of your own, and then write her response

Question

_____
_____
_____
_____
_____
_____
_____

Answer

_____
_____
_____
_____
_____
_____
_____
_____

Raised by wild animals

The boat was thrown upon the beach, and the children were rolled out upon the sand. The neighbouring thickets soon resounded with their mournful cries. A mother wolf who was sleeping there came out to see what was the matter. The wolf caressed the helpless babes, and lying down by their side she cherished and fed them, watching all the time with a fierce and vigilant eye for any approaching enemy or danger.

(*Romulus* by Jacob Abbot)

Write a story about a human baby raised by a family of wild animals.

Questions to think about before you write

- What type of animal will raise this baby?
- Does the child learn to communicate like the animals?
- Does the child learn to eat the same food as the anim
- What do the child's animal brothers and sisters think about their human sibling?

Romulus and Remus

Romulus and Remus were the twin sons of Rhea, the daughter of the king of Alba Longa, who had been overthrown by his son, Amulius. Rhea was a vestal virgin, a young woman who was forbidden to marry or have children. Despite this, she became pregnant. Her children, the twin boys Romulus and Remus, had a right to the throne, so King Amulius, their uncle, had them thrown into the River Tiber to die. Luckily for the children, the shepherd, Faustulus, who was given the job of getting rid of the children, gave them a chance of life by putting them into a small boat.

When they were young men Romulus and Remus found out who they really were and took action. They killed their uncle, King Amulius, and reinstated their grandfather on the throne. They then planned to build a city, but argued about who should be its ruler. During their quarrel, Romulus killed his brother and went on to become king of the new city, which he called Rome.

Rudyard Kipling's famous story, *The Jungle Book*, also features a human who is raised by a pack of wolves.

Stories to believe in

The myths that are included in this book once formed part of strong belief systems held by people from different times in history and in different countries around the world. To them they weren't just stories being passed down the generations, they were telling of real events, featuring gods, demi-gods and mortals, that they truly believed in.

Standing Stones

Around the world there are mysterious sites of standing stones. Perhaps the most famous is Stonehenge in England. It is around 5,000 years old, but as there are no markings on the stones and no other written records, nobody really knows what it was for. What do you think it was used for?

A Painful Ritual

In Mayan ceremonies a ruler, such as a king or a queen, sometimes took part in a blood-letting rite to communicate with their gods. A rope of thorns would be pulled through the worshipper's tongue to pierce it and allow their blood to flow.

Who to Worship

Many people would form a strong attachment to a particular god whom they felt had a significant influence over their life, and who could be important to their survival. Gods associated with crops and the harvest were popular with farmers, for example. Egyptian farmers held a harvest festival each year dedicated to the goddess of plenty, Renenutet, in which they dedicated a portion of their best produce to her, whereas the Greeks would sacrifice a pregnant pig to their goddess of corn and the harvest, Demeter.

Many Romans worshipped household gods, known as Lares, who were believed to protect and influence a specific location, such as a domestic home.

Where to Worship

From sacred lakes to elaborate temples, there were many different places to worship the many gods of ancient mythologies.

In Iceland and Norway it was quite normal for a site of natural beauty, often not even marked with a monument, to be a place to worship the Norse gods.

Temples, such as those in Greece and Egypt, could be complex places. The exterior walls of the Temple of Amun, at Karnak in Egypt, for example, enclosed many smaller temples, and even a lake.

Places of worship were often built on high ground, or if that wasn't possible, on top of a platform, like the pyramids of the Mayans. Many people believed that the realm of the gods was in the sky, so they wanted to conduct their rituals and ceremonies as close to the gods as possible.

Top ancient sites of worship still standing today

Pyramids of the Sun and Moon, Teotihuacán, Mexico

Parthenon, Acropolis, Greece

Stonehenge, Wiltshire, England

Karnak Temple, Luxor, Egypt

Pantheon, Rome, Italy

Ziggurat, Ur, Iraq

A tale of two seasons

So much did Demeter suffer, that she gave herself no trouble about seed time nor harvest. The farmers plowed and planted as usual; but there lay the rich black furrows, all as barren as a desert of sand. "If the earth is ever again to see any vegetation," she said, "it must first grow along the path which my daughter will tread in coming back to me."

(*Tanglewood Tales* by Nathaniel Hawthorne)

Write your own version of the end of this story, from the daughter Persephone's point of view

_____

_____

_____

_____

_____

_____

_____

_____

Questions to think about before you write

- Is Persephone happy or sad in the Underworld?
- Does Persephone want to come home to her mother?
- Did Persephone eat the pomegranate seeds by choice?
- How does Persephone feel about the deal her father strikes with Hades?

Myths often include stories which attempt to explain the world around us. The myth of Demeter and Persephone explains the difference between the seasons of summer and winter.

The Myth of Demeter and Persephone

Persephone was the daughter of Demeter, goddess of corn and the harvest, and Zeus. Hades, god of the Underworld, fell in love with Persephone and wanted her for his wife. One day Hades snatched Persephone and dragged her down to the Underworld. Demeter was so sad and angry about the loss of her daughter that the Earth became cold and crops no longer grew. She persuaded Zeus to take action to rescue their daughter. Zeus came to an agreement with Hades that he would release Persephone, on the condition that she hadn't eaten anything while in the Underworld. Unfortunately it was discovered that she had eaten six pomegranate seeds and that meant a compromise had to be found. For six months of the year she would live on Earth with her mother. During this happy time the world was sunny and warm, and crops would grow. For the other six months of the year she returned to Hades, during which time her mother mourned, Earth turned cold, and nothing grew.

DID YOU KNOW?

In Roman myths, Demeter, the goddess of grain, was known as Ceres. Can you guess what breakfast food is named after her?

Letters of love

"Help me!" she cried. "Save me from him whose love I fear!"

As she spoke the arms of Apollo seized her, yet, even as his arms met around her waist, Daphne the nymph was Daphne the nymph no longer. Her fragrant hair, her soft white arms, her tender body all changed as the sun-god touched them. Her feet took root in the soft, damp earth by the river. Her arms sprouted into woody branches and green leaves. Her face vanished, and the bark of a big laurel tree enclosed her snow-white body. Apollo knew that her cry to Zeus had been answered.

(The Book of Myths by Jean Lang)

Apollo and Daphne

Apollo, the sun god, loved Daphne, but she did not return his love. The more he chased her, the more she ran. Eventually she appealed to Zeus to transform her into something that would save her from Apollo's advances. Zeus answered her prayers and turned her into a laurel tree. Apollo then made a wreath from the leaves of the tree and wore it as a crown.

Write a love letter to someone who dislikes you

Perhaps if Apollo had written a letter to Daphne, rather than chasing her, she might have learnt to return his love. In your letter think about how you might try to persuade the person who dislikes you to give you a chance.

67

An ancient engraving

Ishtar on arriving at the gate of the land of no return,
To the gate-keeper thus addressed herself:

"Gate-keeper, ho, open thy gate!
Open thy gate that I may enter!"

(*The Civilization of Babylonia and Assyria*
by Morris Jastrow Jr)

Ishtar's descent into the Underworld

The goddess Ishtar, who is also known as Inanna, was the Assyrian and Babylonian goddess of fertility. She went to the Underworld to visit her sister, but was stopped from returning to Earth by the demons who lived there. Without Ishtar nothing new grew. There were no new crops, people didn't have babies, and no new animals were born. The god Ea formed a plan to release Ishtar. Once she was back on Earth, life was able to flourish once again.

Imagine you are the archaeologist who found this tablet with writing on it. What story or poem is engraved in the ancient clay?

The poem which tells the story of Ishtar's descent to the Underworld was found on a clay tablet in Nineveh, an ancient Mesopotamian city located in modern-day Iraq. It dates from around 911–612 BC and was excavated by Victorian archaeologist, Sir Austen Henry Layard in the mid-nineteenth century. It's now part of the collection of the British Museum.

Love at first sight

> "I love Guinevere," said King Arthur, "as I think that damsel is the gentlest and the fairest lady living."
>
> (*The Legends of King Arthur and His Knights* by James Knowles)

It's possible that stories about Arthur were first told nearly 2,000 years ago. Although it's likely that the earliest stories were told about a real person, over time he became a figure of legend, and many authors added to his story. Characters such as the wizard, Merlin, and the knight, Lancelot, were introduced, along with the famous Round Table and the sword, Excalibur.

One of the most famous versions of Arthur's story is Alfred Lord Tennyson's poem, "The Passing of Arthur", which he wrote in 1842.

Questions to think about before you write

- Is your story set in ancient times or in the present day?
- What do they do on their first date?
- Does the date go well?

Write your own story of love

Questions to think about before you write

- Will your main characters be gods or mortals?
- Will it have a happy ending, or will it end in tragedy?

TOP TIP

Daydream! You don't need to start writing straight away. Take your time and let your mind wander. You can jot down notes about your story at any time.

Can you work out which mythological characters
are hiding in these anagrams?

DEAR HOP IT

☐☐☐☐☐☐☐☐☐

TRAUMA SEA

☐☐☐☐☐☐☐☐☐

LA LOOP

☐☐☐☐☐☐

EVEN URGE I

☐☐☐☐☐☐☐☐☐

SPHERE OPEN

☐☐☐☐☐☐☐☐☐☐☐

SLUM OUR

☐☐☐☐☐☐☐

HI STAR

☐☐☐☐☐☐

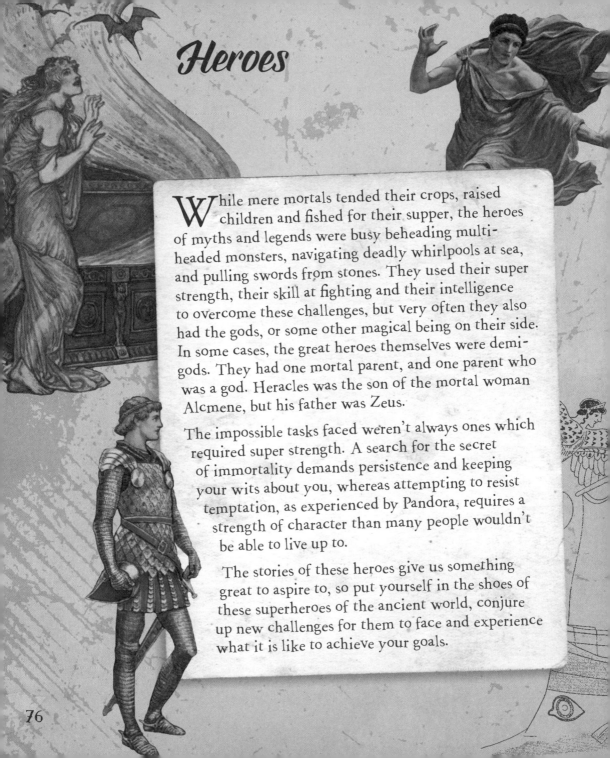

Heroes

While mere mortals tended their crops, raised children and fished for their supper, the heroes of myths and legends were busy beheading multi-headed monsters, navigating deadly whirlpools at sea, and pulling swords from stones. They used their super strength, their skill at fighting and their intelligence to overcome these challenges, but very often they also had the gods, or some other magical being on their side. In some cases, the great heroes themselves were demi-gods. They had one mortal parent, and one parent who was a god. Heracles was the son of the mortal woman Alcmene, but his father was Zeus.

The impossible tasks faced weren't always ones which required super strength. A search for the secret of immortality demands persistence and keeping your wits about you, whereas attempting to resist temptation, as experienced by Pandora, requires a strength of character than many people wouldn't be able to live up to.

The stories of these heroes give us something great to aspire to, so put yourself in the shoes of these superheroes of the ancient world, conjure up new challenges for them to face and experience what it is like to achieve your goals.

Top 5 mythical superheroes

Hercules (known as Heracles in Greek myths)

Kintaro

Gilgamesh

Beowulf

Finn mac Cool

DID YOU KNOW?

The phrase, Herculean task, means needing great strength to complete, and is named after the Greek hero, Hercules who was famous for his physical power.

Diary of a superhero

The second task of Heracles was to destroy a hydra or water snake which dwelt in the marsh of Lerna. The body of this snake was large and from its body sprang nine heads. Eight of these heads were mortal, but the ninth head was undying.

(Heroes Every Child Should Know by Hamilton Wright Mabie)

Draw a picture of your monster here

Create a new monster for Heracles to fight, and write a diary account of how he overcomes the beast

From man-eating birds, to a three-headed guard-dog, to a dragon with a hundred heads, Heracles encountered many strange beasts. Could your monster be even more unreal? Perhaps it's an alien from outer space?

The twelve labours of Heracles

Heracles was set twelve seemingly impossible tasks by King Eurystheus. Each time Heracles was expected to fail and die in his attempt, but each time he surprised the king by completing the challenge, mostly by using his great strength.

What's in the box?

Just imagine how busy your wits would be, if there were a great box in the house, which, as you might have reason to suppose, contained something new and pretty for your Christmas gifts. Do you think that you should be less curious than Pandora? If you were left alone with the box, might you not feel a little tempted to lift the lid?

(*A Wonder-Book for Girls and Boys* by Nathaniel Hawthorne)

You are sitting in a room with a curious box that you have been told not to open. Write the story of what happens next …

What is the box like?

big   small

old   new

decorated   plain

interesting   boring

wooden   metal

heavy   light

A sword's story

There was seen in the churchyard a huge square stone having a naked sword stuck in the midst of it. And on the sword was written in letters of gold, "Whoso pulleth out the sword from this stone is born the rightful King of Britain." Then many knights and barons pulled at the sword with all their might, and some of them tried many times, but none could stir or move it.

(*The Legends of King Arthur and His Knights* by James Knowles)

Write the story of *The Sword in the Stone* from the point of view of the sword

_____

_____

_____

_____

_____

_____

_____

Questions to think about before you write

■ Who will try to pull the sword out of the stone?

■ How does the sword feel?

■ Will Arthur succeed in your story, or perhaps someone else will become King or Queen of Britain?

Superheroes

Do you have a favourite superhero? Spiderman? Wonder Woman? If you don't have a favourite already, you could look at ancient myths to find a superhero to admire. Myths and legends are full of characters who could be superheroes. From gods who can create thunder with their weapons, to goddesses who can turn people into spiders, to demi-gods who have the strength to defeat the most terrifying monsters.

Stories of heroism inspire people to greatness, to be the best they can be. Heroes aren't always found on a battlefield, or saving someone from a fire. A hero can be the runner-up in a race, as long as that's the fastest time they've ever run, or a hero can be someone who helps a friend in need.

List your top 5 superheroes

1. ....
2. ....
3. ....
4. ....
5. ....

What qualities does a mythical superhero have?

Super-strength

Bravery

Talent, for example being a master with a bow and arrow

A god, goddess or other magical being on their side

Draw a picture of
their superhero
costume here

Real name

....

Likes

....

Dislikes

....

Favourite animal

....

Favourite film

....

Favourite song

....

Special powers

....

Weaknesses

....

Superhero name

....

A superhero's story

Using the superhero you created on the previous page, write a story about how they attempt to overcome one or more of the challenges faced by some famous mythical heroes

List of challenges

Kill the multi-headed Hydra

Tame Cerberus, the three-headed guard-dog of the Underworld

Escape a prison built in a labyrinth

Slay Medusa, a gorgon who could turn men to stone with her gaze

Classic comic-book words to include in your story

POW

KABOOM

ROAAAAR

SPLAT

SUDDENLY

THEN

FINALLY

Inspire a hero

"To strive, to seek, to find and not to yield."
("Ulysses" by Alfred Lord Tennyson)

This is the final line from Tennyson's poem, "Ulysses". It was engraved at the entrance to the athletes' village in London's Olympic Park to inspire the athletes of the 2012 Olympics.

The *Odyssey*

The many heroic deeds of Odysseus, known by the Romans as Ulysses, were first told in Homer's epic poem, the *Odyssey*. Odysseus was a soldier making his way back home to his wife, but on his journey he faced many challenges including the Cyclops, greedy giants with a single eye in the centre of their foreheads, the Sirens, whose song lured sailors to their deaths, the six-headed monster, Scylla, and a deadly whirlpool created by the monster, Charybdis. Tennyson's poem, "Ulysses", also told his story.

Write a poem to inspire one of your favourite heroes

List your top 5 real-life heroes

1. ....

2. ....

3. ....

4. ....

5. ....

A tale of immortality

Gilgamesh had been stricken by disease. He wept and cried out, "Oh! let me not die like Ea-bani, for death is fearful." Gilgamesh set out on his journey to obtain the Water of Life and the Plant of Life.

(*Myths of Babylonia and Assyria* by Donald Alexander Mackenzie)

On his quest the hero, Gilgamesh, is cured of his disease, but does not become immortal. Only the gods are able to live forever.

Questions to think about before you write

■ How did you become immortal?

■ Is everyone around you immortal or are you the only one?

I am immortal.

Write your own story of heroes and impossible tasks

This chapter has seen heroes succeed and heroes fail as they try to achieve the seemingly impossible. Will your story end in success or failure?

TOP TIP
Create a world cloud for each of the following elements of your story before you start writing.

Main character

Setting

Challenge

Turn the page for more room to write

Answers

Page 15
a) Salmon

Page 16
Trident - Poseidon
Winged sandals - Hermes
Arrows - Eros
Shield - Athena
Armour - Achilles

Page 47

Crocodile	Sobek, the crocodile god
Cow	Hathor, the goddess of fertility
Falcon	Horus, the god of the sky
Hippopotamus	Taweret, the mother goddess
Cat	Bastet, the goddess of sexuality
Ibis	Thoth, the god of wisdom

Page 53

Crossword answers:
1. P PROTEUS (down)
2. TRITON
3. GRENDEL (down)
4. HYDRA
5. MEDUSA (down)
6. CYCLOPS (down)
7. CENTAUR
8. VAMPIRE
9. SOBEK
CERBERUS (down)

Page 33

Word search grid:
GILGAMESH
PI / SO / RE / RE
JUPITER
ODIN
KUDRAM

Page 75
DEAR HOP IT
APHRODITE

TRAUMA SEA
AMATERASU

LA LOOP
APOLLO

EVEN URGE I
GUINEVERE

SPHERE OPEN
PERSEPHONE

SLUM OUR
ROMULUS

HI STAR
ISHTAR